Jr. Graphic African-Ameri

Crispus Attucks
and the Boston Massacre

PowerKiDS
press

New York

Lynne Weiss

Published in 2014 by The Rosen Publishing Group, Inc.
29 East 21st Street, New York, NY 10010

First Edition

Editor: Joanne Randolph

Book Design: Planman Technologies

Illustrations: Planman Technologies

Library of Congress Cataloging-in-Publication Data

Weiss, Lynne, 1952–

Crispus Attucks and the Boston Massacre / by Lynne Weiss. — First edition.

    pages cm. — (Jr. graphic African-American history)

Includes index.

ISBN 978-1-4777-1315-0 (library binding) — ISBN 978-1-4777-1455-3 (pbk.) — ISBN 978-1-4777-1456-0 (6-pack)

1. Attucks, Crispus, d. 1770—Juvenile literature. 2. African Americans—Biography—Juvenile literature. 3. Revolutionaries—Massachusetts—Boston—Biography—Juvenile literature. 4. Boston Massacre, 1770—Juvenile literature. 5. Attucks, Crispus, d. 1770—Comic books, strips, etc. 6. African Americans—Biography—Comic books, strips, etc. 7. Revolutionaries—Massachusetts—Boston—Biography—Comic books, strips, etc. 8. Boston Massacre, 1770—Comic books, strips, etc. 9. Graphic novels. I. Title.

E185.97.A86W45 2014

973.3'113092—dc23

[B]

2012050198

Manufactured in the United States of America

CPSIA Compliance Information: Batch #WR412180RC: For Further Information contact Rosen Publishing, New York, New York at 1-800-237-9932

Contents

Introduction

Crispus Attucks was the first man to be shot in the cause of American liberty. He escaped slavery and then worked on whaling ships that sailed from Massachusetts. On the night of the Boston **Massacre**, Crispus Attucks joined the cause of **colonial** protesters. The story of his life illustrates the role of African Americans and working people in the struggle for American independence.

Main Characters

Crispus Attucks (c. 1723–1770) African-American worker who was killed in the Boston Massacre.

Samuel Gray (1718–1770) Boston **ropewalker** who was killed in the Boston Massacre.

Paul Revere (1734–1818) **Engraver** of the Boston Massacre scene.

John Adams (1735–1826) **Attorney** in the Boston Massacre trial.

CRISPUS ATTUCKS AND THE BOSTON MASSACRE

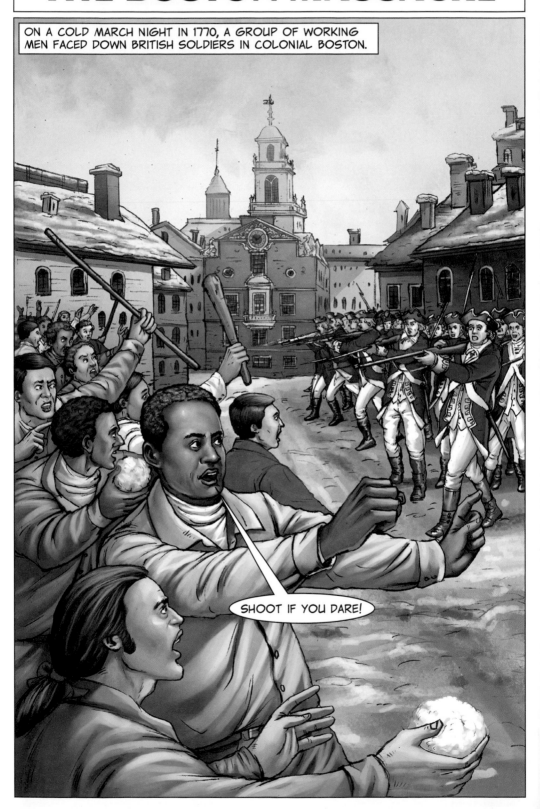

ON A COLD MARCH NIGHT IN 1770, A GROUP OF WORKING MEN FACED DOWN BRITISH SOLDIERS IN COLONIAL BOSTON.

SHOOT IF YOU DARE!

FEELINGS RAN HIGH. THE SITUATION WAS DANGEROUS.

CAPTAIN PRESTON! ORDER YOUR MEN BACK TO THEIR TENTS!

IF THEY BOTHER ME, I WILL FIRE!

THEY DARE NOT FIRE.

CRISPUS ATTUCKS DOVE TOWARD THE SOLDIERS AND THREW HIS CLUB AT THEM. IN RETURN, THE **MUSKETS** ROARED.

ATTUCKS WAS THE FIRST MAN SHOT AT THE EVENT KNOWN AS THE BOSTON MASSACRE. TODAY, MANY PEOPLE CALL HIM THE FIRST HERO IN THE AMERICAN REVOLUTION. WHO WAS THIS MAN?

CRISPUS ATTUCKS WAS BORN ABOUT 1723. HIS FATHER, PRINCE, WAS AN ENSLAVED MAN. HIS MOTHER WAS A NATICK INDIAN. CRISPUS WENT TO SCHOOL AS A CHILD. THEN HE WAS FORCED INTO SLAVERY.

STRONG AND SMART, ATTUCKS BECAME AN EXPERT TRADER IN HORSES AND CATTLE.

SIR, THIS LOOKS LIKE A VERY GOOD HORSE. YOU WOULD BE WISE TO TAKE IT.

ALTHOUGH ATTUCKS WAS A SLAVE, PEOPLE SOMETIMES PAID HIM FOR HIS ADVICE. HE SAVED THE MONEY HE EARNED.

CRISPUS, YOU HAVE NEVER BEEN WRONG. I DO NOT MIND PAYING YOU.

MR. BROWN, I HAVE BEEN SAVING MY MONEY. I WANT TO BUY MY FREEDOM.

CRISPUS, YOU ARE ONE OF MY BEST WORKERS. I CANNOT LET YOU GO. YOU KNOW I WILL ALWAYS TREAT YOU WELL.

I DO NOT WANT TO BE TREATED WELL. I WANT *FREEDOM!*

UNABLE TO BUY HIS FREEDOM, ATTUCKS ESCAPED.

MR. BROWN TOOK OUT A NOTICE IN THE NEWSPAPER AND OFFERED A REWARD.

THE NEW

Ran away from his master: Crispus, about 27 years old, 6 feet 2 inches high. Short, curled hair. Had on light-colored bearskin coat. Whoever returns him shall have 10 pounds

THE REWARD WAS NEVER COLLECTED.

ATTUCKS CHANGED HIS NAME TO MICHAEL JOHNSON AND WENT TO NEW BEDFORD, MASSACHUSETTS.

I AM STRONG AND HARDWORKING. WILL YOU HIRE ME?

WE ALWAYS NEED STRONG, BRAVE MEN ON OUR WHALING SHIPS. IF YOU CATCH A LOT OF WHALES, YOU WILL MAKE EXTRA MONEY.

QUAKERS, MEMBERS OF A RELIGIOUS GROUP THAT WANTED TO END SLAVERY, OWNED MOST WHALING SHIPS. THEY HIRED MANY AFRICAN AMERICANS.

WHALE OIL WAS AN IMPORTANT FUEL BEFORE COAL AND OIL WERE DISCOVERED.

THIS WHALE-OIL LAMP IS MUCH BRIGHTER THAN CANDLES. I NEED THIS LAMP TO DO MY READING AND WRITING.

WHALE OIL WAS USED TO MAKE SOAP AND PAINT. IT WAS ALSO USED TO **LUBRICATE** MACHINE PARTS.

WORK ON WHALING SHIPS WAS HARD. VOYAGES LASTED FOR YEARS. CHASING AND KILLING THE HUGE WHALES WAS DANGEROUS.

ANOTHER DANGER WAS **IMPRESSMENT**. BRITISH SHIPS SOMETIMES STOPPED COLONIAL SHIPS AND FORCED THE SAILORS TO WORK FOR THEM.

ATTUCKS WAS PROMOTED A COUPLE OF TIMES AND BECAME A **BOATSWAIN**.

MAKE SURE YOU WIND THOSE ROPES PROPERLY.

FOR A TIME, ATTUCKS LIVED IN A FREE BLACK COMMUNITY IN THE BAHAMAS.

WE HAVE NO SLAVERY IN THIS TOWN. BLACK PEOPLE RUN EVERYTHING.

I LIKE LIVING HERE. EVERYONE IS FREE.

Florida

Miami

The Bahamas

THEN, IN 1769, HE WENT BACK TO MASSACHUSETTS TO LOOK FOR WORK.

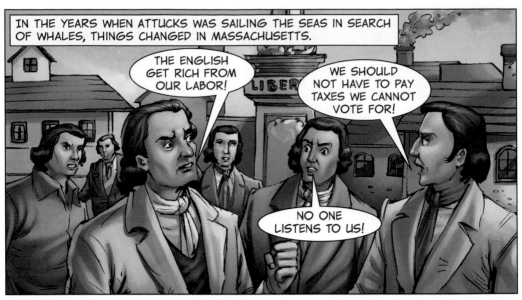

IN THE YEARS WHEN ATTUCKS WAS SAILING THE SEAS IN SEARCH OF WHALES, THINGS CHANGED IN MASSACHUSETTS.

THE ENGLISH GET RICH FROM OUR LABOR!

WE SHOULD NOT HAVE TO PAY TAXES WE CANNOT VOTE FOR!

NO ONE LISTENS TO US!

BRITAIN'S **LAWMAKERS** NEEDED TO RAISE MONEY. THEY WANTED PEOPLE IN THE COLONIES TO PAY NEW TAXES ON THINGS THEY USED EVERY DAY, SUCH AS PRINTED ITEMS AND TEA.

I WILL NOT BUY A NEWSPAPER IF I HAVE TO PAY THIS TAX.

PEOPLE PROTESTED ALL OVER THE COLONIES, BUT THE PROTESTS IN BOSTON WERE THE WORST. TO PUNISH THE PEOPLE OF BOSTON, BRITISH WARSHIPS ARRIVED IN BOSTON HARBOR IN 1768.

THE SHIPS CARRIED SOLDIERS TO **OCCUPY** THE CITY OF BOSTON. SOON THE STREETS OF BOSTON WERE FILLED WITH BRITISH TROOPS.

IT MAKES MY BLOOD BOIL TO SEE THOSE **REDCOATS** MARCHING THROUGH OUR STREETS.

SOME PEOPLE IN BOSTON WERE FORCED TO LET SOLDIERS LIVE IN THEIR HOMES. THEY HAD TO FEED THEM, TOO.

MEN AND BOYS FROM SURROUNDING TOWNS CAME TO BOSTON TO FIGHT THE SOLDIERS. THEY WERE NOT AN ORGANIZED ARMY, BUT THEY WERE ANGRY.

THEY ARE STEALING FROM US AND WRECKING OUR HOMES.

I HEARD ONE OF THEM ATTACKED A LADY CARRYING A BIBLE.

WE NEED TO DRIVE THEM OUT!

THOSE WHO WANTED TO GET THE BRITISH OUT OF BOSTON AND THE COLONIES WERE CALLED **PATRIOTS**.

FIGHTS BROKE OUT BETWEEN THE PATRIOTS AND BRITISH SOLDIERS.

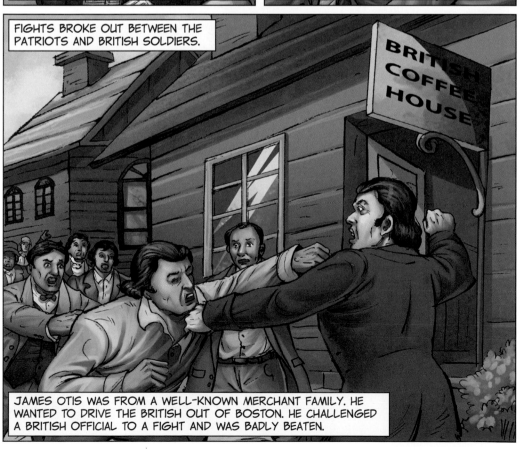

BRITISH COFFEE HOUSE

JAMES OTIS WAS FROM A WELL-KNOWN MERCHANT FAMILY. HE WANTED TO DRIVE THE BRITISH OUT OF BOSTON. HE CHALLENGED A BRITISH OFFICIAL TO A FIGHT AND WAS BADLY BEATEN.

WHEN ATTUCKS CAME BACK TO BOSTON IN THE WINTER OF 1769 TO 1770, HE HOPED TO FIND A JOB ON A SHIP SAILING OUT OF BOSTON HARBOR.

DO YOU HAVE ANY WORK FOR AN EXPERIENCED SAILOR AND WHALE MAN?

BRITISH SHIPS ARE BLOCKING THE HARBOR. HARDLY ANYTHING IS COMING IN OR GOING OUT.

ATTUCKS WENT TO WORK IN A ROPEWALK. WORKERS DID THE DIFFICULT WORK OF MAKING ROPES BY WALKING BACKWARD AND SPINNING **HEMP** FIBERS FOR 12 TO 14 HOURS AT A TIME.

SAMUEL, THEY SAY YOU ARE ONE OF THOSE TRYING TO DRIVE THE BRITISH OUT OF BOSTON.

INDEED I AM.

ROPEWALKERS OFTEN STUCK TOGETHER EVEN WHEN THEY WERE NOT WORKING. THEY CARRIED THEIR BIG WOODEN ROPEWALKING CLUBS WHEN WALKING AROUND TOWN.

WHEN PEOPLE SEE US WITH OUR CLUBS, THEY KNOW TO LEAVE US ALONE. I LIKE IT THAT WAY.

LIFE WAS ALSO HARD FOR THE BRITISH SOLDIERS. THEY WERE PAID SO POORLY THAT THEY HAD TO FIND OTHER JOBS. ON MARCH 3, 1770, ONE SOLDIER CAME TO THE ROPEWALK WHERE ATTUCKS WORKED.

I AM LOOKING FOR SOME WORK.

GRAY'S ROPEWALK

GET OUT OF HERE!

A FIGHT BROKE OUT BETWEEN THE ROPEWALKERS AND THE SOLDIER AND HIS FRIENDS.

MAGISTRATES BROKE IT UP, BUT EVERYONE KNEW THE FIGHT WAS NOT OVER.

13

JUST TWO DAYS LATER, THERE WAS MORE TROUBLE. A WIGMAKER SAID A BRITISH OFFICER HAD NOT PAID FOR HIS WIG. THE WIGMAKER SENT HIS APPRENTICE TO CHASE THE OFFICER DOWN.

YOU DID NOT PAY FOR YOUR WIG!

GET AWAY FROM ME, YOU LITTLE LIAR!

THERE MUST BE A FIRE!

ATTUCKS AND THE ROPEWALKERS KNEW THAT THE FIRE BELL WAS A SIGNAL THAT A FIGHT WAS STARTING.

THAT IS NO FIRE! THAT IS THE SIGNAL TO FIGHT!

PEOPLE CAME RUNNING FROM ALL OVER BOSTON. TEMPERS WERE HIGH. FOR 15 TENSE MINUTES, BRITISH SOLDIERS AND PATRIOTS STARED AT ONE ANOTHER.

SUDDENLY, ATTUCKS THREW HIS CLUB AT ONE OF THE SOLDIERS.. THE BRITISH BEGAN FIRING.

ATTUCKS WAS KILLED, AND SO WAS HIS FRIEND SAMUEL GRAY. THREE OTHER MEN DIED AS WELL.

THE PATRIOTS NAMED THE EVENT THE BOSTON MASSACRE. PAUL REVERE MADE AN ENGRAVING OF IT. HE AND SAMUEL ADAMS PRINTED AND PASSED OUT THOUSANDS OF COPIES. ANGER AT THE BRITISH GREW.

IF THEY ARE GOING TO MASSACRE US, WE MUST FIGHT BACK!

THE FUNERAL FOR CRISPUS ATTUCKS AND THE OTHERS KILLED AT THE MASSACRE WAS HUGE. BOSTON'S POPULATION AT THE TIME WAS ABOUT 15,000, AND THOUSANDS OF PEOPLE ATTENDED THE FUNERAL.

JOHN ADAMS, WHO WOULD LATER BECOME THE SECOND PRESIDENT OF THE UNITED STATES, WAS A PATRIOT. YET HE AGREED TO ACT AS THE ATTORNEY FOR THE BRITISH SOLDIERS.

I WANT TO PROVE THAT LAWS, NOT **MOBS**, RULE THESE COLONIES.

HOWEVER, LAWYERS SOMETIMES MAKE ARGUMENTS THAT EXPRESS VIEWS OTHER THAN THEIR OWN.

ADAMS ARGUED THAT THE SOLDIERS ACTED IN SELF-DEFENSE. ONLY TWO WERE FOUND GUILTY.

ADAMS SENT A LETTER TO NEWSPAPERS THAT ACCUSED THE BRITISH SOLDIERS OF "DELIBERATE" MURDER. HE SIGNED HIS LETTER WITH THE NAME CRISPUS ATTUCKS.

CRISPUS ATTUCKS AND THE OTHERS WHO DIED IN THE BOSTON MASSACRE WERE FORGOTTEN FOR MANY YEARS. IN 1858, A **COMMEMORATION** WAS HELD IN BOSTON.

WHO TAUGHT THE BRITISH SOLDIER THAT HE MIGHT BE DEFEATED? WHO DARED FIRST TO LOOK INTO HIS EYES? CRISPUS ATTUCKS IS FOREMOST OF MEN WHO DARED.

AFRICAN AMERICANS IN BOSTON BEGAN TO OBSERVE CRISPUS ATTUCKS DAY ON MARCH 5. IN 1888, A MONUMENT WAS PLACED ON BOSTON COMMON.

CRISPUS ATTUCKS WAS THE FIRST PERSON SHOT IN THE BOSTON MASSACRE AND BECAME A **MARTYR** OF THE AMERICAN REVOLUTION.

HE WAS RECKLESS, BUT HE WAS BRAVE, TOO.

HE WAS ALWAYS SEEKING FREEDOM.

ATTUCKS WAS NOT THE ONLY AFRICAN AMERICAN WHO TOOK PART IN THE AMERICAN REVOLUTION. SOME ENSLAVED MEN WERE PROMISED FREEDOM IF THEY FOUGHT FOR THE UNITED STATES. PETER SALEM WAS ONE OF SEVERAL AFRICAN-AMERICAN MEN WHO FOUGHT AT LEXINGTON IN THE FIRST BATTLE OF THE REVOLUTION.

AT THE BATTLE OF BUNKER HILL, AN AFRICAN-AMERICAN NAMED SALEM POOR SHOT AND KILLED THE BRITISH COMMANDER, MAJOR PITCAIRN. HE WAS PRESENTED TO GENERAL GEORGE WASHINGTON AS A HERO.

SALEM POOR WAS SO HEROIC THAT 14 AMERICAN OFFICERS ASKED CONGRESS TO REWARD THIS "BRAVE AND GALLANT" SOLDIER.

ONE OF THE MOST FAMOUS PAINTINGS OF THE AMERICAN REVOLUTION SHOWS AN AFRICAN-AMERICAN MAN IN THE BOAT WITH GEORGE WASHINGTON.

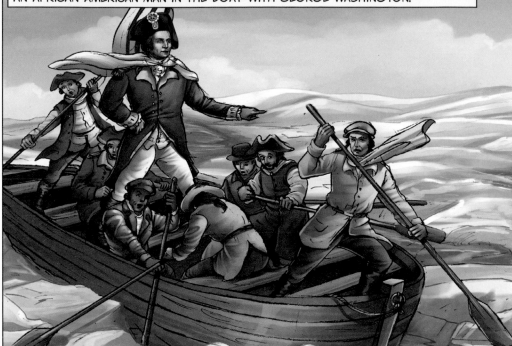

SOME HISTORIANS BELIEVE THIS MAN WAS PRINCE WHIPPLE. WHIPPLE TOOK PART IN MANY BATTLES DURING THE WAR AND SIGNED A PETITION TO END SLAVERY IN HIS HOME STATE OF NEW HAMPSHIRE.

AGRIPPA HULL WAS BORN FREE IN MASSACHUSETTS. HE JOINED THE CONTINENTAL ARMY IN 1777. HE WAS AN AIDE TO GENERAL WASHINGTON'S CHIEF ENGINEER.

A HARDWORKING FARMER AND CAREFUL MANAGER, HULL BECAME ONE OF THE WEALTHIEST LANDOWNERS IN STOCKBRIDGE, MASSACHUSETTS, AFTER THE WAR.

THE CAPTAIN OFFERED ME MY FREEDOM IF I WOULD GO LIVE IN ENGLAND. I REFUSED. I DID NOT WANT TO BE A TRAITOR.

JAMES FORTEN, A 15-YEAR-OLD PHILADELPHIA NATIVE, VOLUNTEERED TO SERVE ON AN AMERICAN SHIP. THE BRITISH LATER CAPTURED IT. FORTEN SPENT SEVEN MONTHS AS A PRISONER OF WAR.

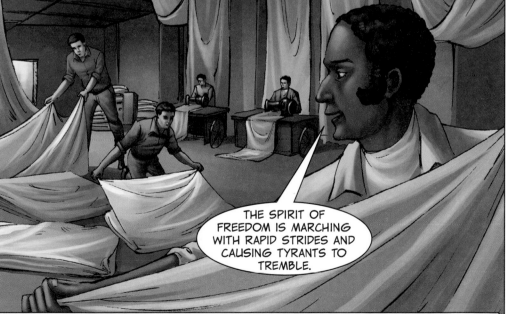

AFTER THE WAR, FORTEN MADE A FORTUNE MAKING SAILS FOR SHIPS. HE TRIED TO END SLAVERY AND WIN RIGHTS FOR WOMEN AND POOR PEOPLE.

THE SPIRIT OF FREEDOM IS MARCHING WITH RAPID STRIDES AND CAUSING TYRANTS TO TREMBLE.

FORTEN LIVED TO SEE HIS CHILDREN AND GRANDCHILDREN BECOME LEADERS IN THE **ABOLITIONIST** CRUSADE THAT FINALLY ENDED SLAVERY FOR ALL AFRICAN AMERICANS. CRISPUS ATTUCKS WOULD HAVE BEEN PROUD TO SEE HIS DESIRE FOR FREEDOM FINALLY COME TO PASS IN THE NATION HE SERVED WITH SUCH BRAVERY AND HONOR.

Timeline

1718	Samuel Gray is born in Rhode Island.
1723	Crispus Attucks is born in Massachusetts.
1750	Crispus Attucks escapes from slavery.
1765	The Stamp Act taxes all printed items sold in the colonies. Protests begin.
1768	British troops occupy Boston.
1769	Crispus Attucks returns to Boston.
March 5, 1770	Crispus Attucks and Samuel Gray are killed in the Boston Massacre.
December 5, 1770	End of the Boston Massacre trial. Two soldiers are found guilty, and six are acquitted.
December 16, 1773	Boston Tea Party. Patriots dump over 300 chests of tea into Boston Harbor to protest British tax policies.
June 1774	Quartering Act. The colonies are forced, by law, to provide housing for British soldiers.
July 4, 1776	The Declaration of Independence is adopted.
October 1781	British troops surrender at Yorktown, Virginia. This is the last battle of the Revolutionary War.
September 1783	The United States and Britain sign the Treaty of Paris, officially ending the Revolutionary War.
March 5, 1858	Crispus Attucks Day is held to commemorate the Boston Massacre.
1865	The Thirteenth Amendment, which abolished slavery in the United States, is ratified.
1888	The Boston Massacre memorial statue is erected on Boston Common.

Glossary

abolitionist (a-buh-LIH-shun-ist) Someone who worked to end slavery.

attorney (uh-TUR-nee) A person who goes to court to prove that someone has broken the law or who defends a person's actions. Also known as a lawyer.

boatswain (BOH-sun) A sailor responsible for supervising work related to maintenance of the hull of a ship.

colonial (kuh-LOH-nee-ul) Having to do with the period of time when the United States was made of 13 colonies ruled by England.

commemoration (kuh-MEH-muh-ray-shun) An official remembrance.

engraver (en-GRAYV-er) Someone who designs pictures that are cut into wood, stone, metal, or glass plates for printing.

hemp (HEMP) A tall Asian herb widely grown for its tough woody fiber that is used to make rope.

impressment (im-PRES-ment) The act of forcing someone into service.

lawmakers (LAW-may-kurz) People who write and pass laws.

lubricate (LOO-bruh-kayt) To make smooth or slippery.

magistrates (MA-jih-strayts) Officials who make sure that laws are obeyed.

martyr (MAR-ter) Someone who dies or is killed for a cause or a principle.

massacre (MA-sih-ker) The act of killing a large number of people or animals.

mobs (MOBZ) Large, rowdy crowds.

muskets (MUS-kits) Long-barreled firearms used by soldiers before the invention of the rifle.

occupy (AH-kyuh-py) To take or hold possession or control of.

Patriots (PAY-tree-uts) American colonists who believed in separating from British rule.

pounds (POWNDZ) English money. One pound was equal to 20 shillings or 100 pennies.

Quakers (KWAY-kurz) People who belong to a faith that believes in equality for all people, strong families and communities, and peace.

redcoats (RED-kohts) Slang term for British soldiers because of these soldiers' bright red uniform coats.

ropewalker (ROHP-wawk-er) A person who makes rope.

Index

Websites

Due to the changing nature of Internet links, PowerKids Press has developed an online list of websites related to the subject of this book. This site is updated regularly. Please use this link to access the list:

www.powerkidslinks.com/jgaah/crispus/